Th

MW00852506

1

The Law of the Tongue

"The Laws of the Kingdom Series"

Kingdom Law Book III

The Law of the Tongue

Understanding The Authority and Power of Speaking in the Kingdom

Dr. J.C. Matthews

Another anointed book from:

**BLESSED BOOKS
PUBLISHING CO.**

P.O. Box 360102

Irving, Texas 75063

www.blessedbookspublishing.com

ISBN 978-0-9792554-6-5

Printed in the United States of America

Blessed Books Publishing Company

Visit or site at: www.blessedbookspublishing.com

Table of Contents

The Law of the Tongue

The Law of the Tongue

In the Beginning ...

*"In the beginning God created the heavens and
the earth' ... 'And God said ..."*
Genesis 1:1-3 NIV

In the beginning *"God said ... "*. In the Book of
Beginnings God is revealed as The Speaking Spirit. One
who creates, not from physical material but from His
words. The Bible records all throughout Genesis chapter
one that *"God said"*, and then *He saw* what He said.
God's words were more than sounds resonating through
the air but the substance and foundational material that
comprised everything that was created. God's word is

the medium by which His thoughts are introduced into our physical world and become the things that fill it. The thoughts God had concerning the earth, He placed within His Words. Through the act of speaking, God releases into the physical world, intangible substance whose assignment it was to manifest itself in the earth.

This creative act of speaking is so closely related to who God is that the Bible identifies God as being "The Word". In the Gospel of John, the Holy Spirit reveals this to us through the writings of the Apostle John:

> *"In the beginning was the Word, and the Word was with God, and the Word was God. He was in the beginning with God. All things were made through Him, and without Him nothing was made that was made".* [1]

Also:

> *"By faith we understand that the worlds were framed by the word of God, so that the things which are seen were not made of things which are visible."* [2]

---

[1] John 1:1-4
[2] Hebrews 11:3

The Bible is clear that every tangible thing that exists in this world came from God's word. This creative Word by God subsequently revealed itself to be Jesus the Christ, who became a man in order to redeem all of mankind. However, He was first introduced to us as the *"Word of God"*, through whom all things were created.

Not only were the tangible things created by God's Word but the intangible and spiritual things as well. We are told in the book of Colossians:

> *"For by Him all things were created that are in heaven and that are on earth, visible and invisible, whether thrones or dominions or principalities or powers. All things were created through Him and for Him. And He is before all things, and in Him all things consist".[3]*

The Psalmist, declares:

> *"By the word of the Lord the heavens were made, and all the host of them by the breath of His mouth".[4]*

---

[3] Colossians 1:16-17
[4] Psalms 33:6

The Bible in Basic English translation, translates this
verse to say:

> *"By the word of the Lord were the heavens
> made; and all the army of heaven by the
> breath of his mouth" (BBE)*[5]

This fundamental principle impacts how we are to
perceive God's Word. God's Word comprises all there is
seen and unseen. This truth should govern and impact
our understanding of how God provides for us.

In the Kingdom of God, God provides for His people by
what He says first, not by what we physically possess.
His Word is the provision, upon which all other
manifestation depends.

Universe

It is appropriate to note at this point in our study, that
the word "universe" testifies to this revelation concerning
God's Word being the substance of all things.

---

[5] Id.

The word *"universe"* is a compound word comprised of the words "uni" and "verse". The word "uni" means *one*, and the word "verse" can generically be defined as being, *a string of related words having a common object*. In Genesis chapter two, the Bible says:

> *"Thus the heavens and the earth, and all the host of them, were finished. And on the seventh day God ended His work which He had done, and He rested on the seventh day from all His work which He had done"*[6]

The period at the very end of Genesis chapter 1 indicated that God was finished creating the physical universe. Therefore, Genesis chapter 1 is one verse – or the universe.

Every resource man would ever need to experience fullness in life and to fulfill his purpose was created. God is not going to create more of anything for us. The Bible says that He rested or finished speaking creatively. From this point forward, we will see God using that which has already exists to meet our needs. This law

---

[6] Genesis 2:1-2

must be remembered when we are seeking manifestation in our lives.

The Law of "Things"

TRUTH CAN NOT BE SEEN ONLY EVIDENCED

Things, in the truest sense, cannot be seen. We have been trained from a natural standpoint to only consider the things that we can see and touch as being real. This is in error. When we limit our understanding of things being only that which can be touched or seen, we limit ourselves in what we can achieve, believe and receive from God. The Apostle Paul warned us of this error when he wrote:

> *"we do not look at the things which are seen, but at the things which are not seen. For the things which are seen are temporary, but the things which are not seen are eternal".[7]*

In the Kingdom of God, the most important and meaningful "things" we have are things that cannot be

---

[7] 2Corinthians 4:18

seen. The book of Hebrews states, *"without faith it is impossible to please God"*[8] and that *"faith is the substance of things hoped for, the evidence of things not seen"*.[9] In order to fulfill our purpose in life and participate in advancing God's Kingdom, we must be adept at esteeming and handling things that cannot be seen, in particularly God's, and our, words.

How we handle and esteem the unseen things in our lives, will determine what we ultimately see in life. In the Kingdom of God, thoughts are things. The things we see are simply the thoughts that have manifested themselves in time.

The Law of Creation and Manifestation

Laws of a nation work in conjunction with, and in the framework of, other laws that were established to maintain a desired order and provide a predetermined

---

[8] Hebrews 11:6
[9] Hebrews 11:1

outcome. These laws are subject to the influence of related laws, which also must be understood to experience all the benefits afforded by the laws of the land.

Well, the same is true within the Kingdom of God. The Kingdom of God is a government that operates according to principles and laws. There are several laws that impact our ability to properly employ the laws that govern the use of our tongues. Having an understanding of these laws allows us to operate within the laws that govern our words with authority and a knowing confidence. As indicated earlier in this chapter, God's words, although unseen, provided the substance for all that is seen. This revelation must be remembered as we operate within the laws that govern the use of our mouths.

The Difference Between Creation and Manifestation

When we read Genesis chapter 1, we are presented with what is known as the "Creation Account". This is due to the fact that God created everything that exists within this one chapter. However, we must make a significant distinction between when something is created and when it actually manifests. Having an understanding of this distinction allows us to properly interpret certain texts in the Bible that seem illogical due to God, or one of His representatives, speaking of a matter as if it has already happened, when it naturally is yet to occur. This is due to the Law of Creation.

The Law of Creation

The Law of Creation basically says: *All things that are seen have their origin in that which is the unseen.* We referenced this scripture earlier, but it bears repeating for emphasis. The writer of Hebrews said:

"By faith we understand that the worlds were framed by the word of God, so that the things which are seen were not made of things which are visible".[10]

The issue is not whether or not God has provided, but whether what He has provided has manifested yet. Our inability to see a thing does not negate its reality.

This law is demonstrated in Genesis chapter 1 and 2. In Genesis 1 the Bible says that God created the grass of the field, the tress and every herb in the earth. After God finished creating the plant and animal life, He creates man and gives him dominion. Specifically, the text reads:

"Then God said, "Let Us make man in Our image, according to Our likeness; let them have dominion over the fish of the sea, over the birds of the air, and over the cattle, over all the earth and over every creeping thing that creeps on the earth." So God created man in His own image; in the image of God He created him; male and female He created them. Then God blessed them, and God said to them, "Be fruitful and multiply; fill the earth and subdue

---

[10] Hebrews 11:3

22

it; have dominion over the fish of the sea, over the birds of the air, and over every living thing that moves on the earth." And God said, "See, I have given you every herb that yields seed which is on the face of all the earth, and every tree whose fruit yields seed; to you it shall be for food. Also, to every beast of the earth, to every bird of the air, and to everything that creeps on the earth, in which there is life, I have given every green herb for food"; and it was so".[11]

The Bible is clear in verses 26 through 28 that God "created" man. However, we know from scripture, that Adam was not formed until Genesis 2:7 and woman until Genesis 2:22. Therefore, how could the Bible declare, *"God created man, in His image ... male and female He created them"* if it later states that He formed the man and fashioned woman in the very next chapter? The answer lies in the fact that creation is not manifestation. Creation is a spiritual act, while manifestation is a physical one. Let me give you another example, and then we will discuss both of these seeming contradictions from

---

[11] Genesis 1:26-30

the revelation that creation is a spiritual act, while manifestation is a physical one.

The Law of Manifestation

In Genesis chapter 2 the Bible says:

> *"This is the history of the heavens and the earth when they were created, in the day that the Lord God made the earth and the heavens, before any plant of the field was in the earth and before any herb of the field had grown. For the Lord God had not caused it to rain on the earth, and there was no man to till the ground; but a mist went up from the earth and watered the whole face of the ground. And the Lord God formed man of the dust of the ground, and breathed into his nostrils the breath of life; and man became a living being. The Lord God planted a garden eastward in Eden, and there He put the man whom He had formed. And out of the ground the Lord God made every tree grow that is pleasant to the sight and good for food".[12]*

---

[12] Genesis 2:4-9

24

In comparing the language of Genesis chapter 1 and 2 we discover that Genesis 1 concerns the *"creation"* of all things, while Genesis 2 concerns the *"manifestation"* of what was created.

In Genesis 1, the Bible says that God created the grass, trees, herbs and it was so. The phrase, *"it was so"*, means; whatever "God said" came into existence right then and there. The reason God could say *"it was so"* is because He knows that manifestation is not creation, but a fruit of it. Genesis chapter 2, states that nothing had grown in the earth because God had not yet caused it to rain, nor was there a man to till the ground. The substance of the grass, trees and herbs came into existence when the words calling for them were spoken. Their substance simply awaited God's perfect timing to manifest itself in the earth.

When God said, *"Let Us make man ..,"* man came into being when He spoke these words. God's Word established man as a living being. This is seen when God addressed man as both "male and female". In speaking, God not only provided the substance of their being, but their purpose as well. Their differences in purpose did not manifest until God "formed" man and "fashioned" woman from that which was already in existence. The Bible does not say that God created man or woman in Genesis chapter 2 because they were already in existence; they simply had not been given a bodies to manifest themselves in. This is the Law of Manifestation. *OH JESUS THIS DUDE...*

The law of Manifestation requires that God use something physical in order to manifest that which is spiritual in the earth. This is why God had to become a man when He wanted to save man from eternal separation from Him and His Kingdom. God is Spirit, therefore in order for Himself to legally enter the earth and represent man, He needed a body in which to manifest His substance (which is Spirit) in the earth[13]. This is why Genesis chapter one tells us that man was created (male and female), but in chapter two tells us

THE REAL SUBSTANCE IS SPIRIT.

---

[13] John 1:14 and 1John 1:1-2

that God formed Adam (male) and then fashioned Eve (female). He had to place the spirit man into a physical body in order for the man to manifest as a "human" and have dominion in the earth.

I'M FASHIONABLE B/C I WAS FASHIONED

The Law and Order

"And God said ... "

In Genesis chapter 1 we are introduced to the primary law upon which God's spiritual and physical Kingdoms are governed and operated – speaking. Speaking is not only creative, but it is also the means by which the citizens of the Kingdom exercises authority. Words are the common currency between heaven and earth. It impacts the tangible and intangible, the physical and spiritual. Jesus declared that our words are so important and powerful that we are held accountable for every idle word we speak[14].

---

[14] Matthew 12:36

In the very first book and chapter of the Bible, God introduces us to the foundational law the governs His Kingdom and our existence as citizens within His Kingdom.

As a foundation, the number 10 is the number of law. The Bible records the phrase *"God said"* ten times in the very first chapter of the Bible in which He constructed His physical Kingdom in the earth.[15] Therefore, the Kingdom is founded upon "God speaking" and what God says being the law of His Kingdom.

This understanding of God's Word being law is seen when God gave man the Ten Commandments. The Ten Commandments are also known as the "Decalogue". The word Decalogue is comprised of the words "deca" which means 10, and the word "logue" which is derived from the word "logo" which means "word". Therefore, it is literally translated the *"10 words"*. We know that the 10 commandments were comprised of more than just 10

---

[15] Genesis 1:3, 6, 9, 11, 14, 20, 24, 26, 28, 29.

words, but they represented 10 complete thoughts or purposes of God concerning man's government within His Kingdom. From God's perspective the words He speaks are the sum total of the thing spoken of. We do not see God repeating Himself in the creation account because His Words contained everything necessary for them to fulfill their purpose in being spoken.

God's Word concerning a matter contains the thought, substance and purpose for the matter. One word is pregnant with the fulfillment of the thought. Therefore, one word by God may have generations in mind, not just the individual to whom the words was spoken. From a Kingdom perspective, it is not the quantity or volume of the words spoken, but the quality. God's Word is of the highest quality. They are life!

The most important and powerful thing a human being can do is to speak! Words are the common currency between heaven and earth. From a biblical standpoint words are not sounds but *things.* This is why it is so important to understand the significance of our being created in the likeness of God. When Genesis 1:26 says that we were created in the *image and likeness* of God, it does not mean that we look like God. God is spirit and therefore cannot be seen. The Bible's reference to our being created in God's image and likeness is found not in any physical resemblance, but in our ability to function and act like God – primarily by speaking!

Another Speaking Spirit

Speaking is an exercise of authority. By speaking we impact both the seen and unseen worlds. Our words are living substance that outlives us. Once spoken, our words go about the process of manifesting themselves in the lives of the hearer. This is why Jesus warns us that we will give an account for every idle word spoken[16]. Once a word is spoken it impacts its environment and the lives of those it comes into contact with.

---

[16] Matthew 12:36

God granted this power to man as a means and provision for him to exercise dominion in the earth. No other creation has this power. Specifically, Genesis 2:7 says:

> *"And the Lord God formed man of the dust of the ground, and breathed into his nostrils the breath of life; and man became a living being."*

The important and defining revelation in this text is the fact that God "breathed into man's nostrils the breath of life...". The importance of the act of God *breathing* into man the breadth of life, transcends the idea of man becoming alive, but this breadth also creating a "being" or living "soul". The soul is that place in which the mind, intellect and other mental faculties are found. The Hebrew word *"Nashamah"*, used for "*breathed*" and "*breath*" in Genesis 2:7, is also translated as the word *"inspiration"* in the Old Testament. The word inspiration comes from the word "inspire". The Merriam-Webster Online dictionary defines the word "inspire" as meaning: *to influence, move or guide by divine or supernatural means; to breathe or blow into or upon as to give life, and to communicate to an agent*

WHEN GOD BREATH HIS LIFE INTO ME HE TRANSFERRED INTO ME HIS MIND, INTELLECT, AND ALL MENTAL FACULTIES. — WOW

32

supernaturally: to draw forth or bring out thoughts.[17] In the New Testament, the Greek word for the word "inspiration" is *"theoneustros"*[18]. The word *theoneustros* means *God breathed.*

SPEAK GOD THOUGHTS ONLY

Therefore, the breath of God not only gave man life, but the ability to communicate with God and bring forth His thoughts by speaking. God gave man the ability to act and speak on His behalf in the earth, thereby causing the earth to hear its Creator's voice through the voice of His authorized representative. This is how man exercises dominion in the earth.

This fact is further seen in the study of an old Aramaic version of the scriptures called the Targum Onkelos. The Targum Onkelos were written during the time in which the Jews were in exile and had lost the ability to speak their mother tongue due to their being in captivity.   This

---

[17] Merriam-Webster's Online Dictionary - http://www.merriam-webster.com/dictionary/inspire
[18] See 2Timothy 3:16

Aramaic translation of scripture, translates Genesis 2:7 as stating:

> *"And man being a living being"* as: *"And man became another speaking spirit"*.

Man became another speaking spirit like The Speaking Spirit in whose likeness he was created. Therefore, man's dominion was not to be found in his physical abilities, but in his ability to think and speak like God does.

The Power of Naming

The revelation that man's dominion is determined by what he says, is further evidenced by what God required Adam to do once He formed him from the dust of the ground and he became another speaking spirit. The Bible says,

> *"Out of the ground the Lord God formed every beast of the field and every bird of the air, and brought them to Adam to see what he would*

call them. And whatever Adam called each
living creature, that was its name".[19]

The first official act of dominion assigned to Adam was
speaking over God's creatures to give them names. Man
exercises his dominion over God's creation by acting like
God in speaking what God has said concerning a matter.
This is the essence of another Law of the Tongue, which
is known as the Law of Confession, which we will cover
in greater detail later.

What's In a Name?

The Bible says that, whatever Adam called or named a
thing, that was its name. *What power!* The destiny of
the creature brought before Adam was defined by the
words that proceeded out of his mouth. In exercising this
authority, Adam was demonstrating a unique ability
reserved for man that empowers him to fulfill the

---

[19] Genesis 2:19

dominion mandate given him by God. The act of naming a person or thing is an indication of one having authority over the person or thing being named. The declaration and bestowal of names upon another was not only an exercise of authority but an impartation of destiny as well.

This is why God often changed a person's name as they began to enter into their purpose. The name spoken by God over the individual contained the substance of the person's purpose and destiny. For instances, God changed *Abram's* name to *Abraham*, which meant *"father of many nations"*, as confirmation of His promise to prosper him and his seed. God changed Jacob's name (which meant *supplanter*) to Israel, which means *"God prevails"*, after Jacob wrestled with God during night and refused to let Him go until He blessed him. God sent an angel to Mary and Joseph to tell them what they were required to name their child, indicating that God was the child's true Father and the One responsible for naming and imparting destiny to His Son. Jesus changed Simon's name, which meant *"hearing"* to *"Peter"* which

means *"rock"* after Simon received his revelation from
heaven and confessed Jesus as the Son of God. Jesus
declared, "upon this rock I will build my church". That
rock was the revelation and confession of Jesus as the
Son of God. Finally, God changed Saul's name, which
was a very prestigious name in the Jewish community
due it being the name of Israel's first king, to Paul. Paul
is translated to mean "little". This is in part due to the
humbling that Paul would endure to fulfill his purpose.
Paul, who once was a highly esteemed Pharisee within
the Jewish culture, who once persecuted the church, was
transformed into an exile amongst his own people who
ultimately died building the church he once tried to
destroy.

This is why it is so important for us to understand
scripture from a kingdom conscious perspective. We
must understand the dominion and power God has given
us to impact not only our lives but the lives of others with
our words. Scripture testifies that our tongues possess

the power of death and life.[20] Satan has convinced many of us that our words don't matter. Therefore we speak things that we do not mean and thereby reap harvests that we do not want.

Often, we name our children not having the faintest idea of what the name actually means at its origin. We name them after famous personalities, T.V. shows and characters, not knowing that we are imparting destiny upon the person. Some have even named their children after persons or situations that caused them pain, in an attempt to never forget the person or situation. These acts all have spiritual and practical implications in the lives of the one being named.

We see the impact of one's name illustrated in the story of Jabez. In 1 Chronicles chapter 4 we are introduced to a man named Jabez. We are told that Jabez was more honorable than his counterparts but had a name that was contrary to what he perceived as his destiny. The

---

[20] Proverbs 18:21

name Jabez means: *"pain or to cause pain"*. His name was given to him by his mother apparently due to the difficulty she experienced in giving birth to him. Therefore, whenever anyone called his name, they were declaring that he *caused pain*. As Jabez strove to fulfill his purpose in life, he makes a petition to God that reflects his understanding of the impact a name can have upon his destiny. Specifically, 1Chronicles 4:10 says:

> *"And Jabez called on the God of Israel saying, "Oh, that You would bless me indeed, and enlarge my territory, that Your hand would be with me, and that You would keep me from evil, that I may not cause pain!" So God granted him what he requested."*

Jabez concludes his prayer by asking God to frustrate the destiny his name declares. Like Jabez, we must be careful not to receive and accept names that do not agree with what God's Word and purpose for our lives. We must be cognizant of the impact spoke words and names have upon us. They are designed to impart destiny and inform others of who and what we are. Remember, the words we receive in life will be what manifests in our lives.

The Lying Tongue

"These six things the Lord hates, Yes, seven are an abomination to Him: A proud look, A lying tongue, Hands that shed innocent blood, A heart that devises wicked plans, Feet that are swift in running to evil, A false witness who speaks lies, And one who sows discord among brethren." Proverbs 6:16-19

Now that we've discovered the power that God invested in man by creating him as "another speaking spirit", we must also realize that this power carries with it great responsibility. Satan recognizes the power that lies within the tongue and strives to use man's tongue to cause his will, instead of God's will to be done in the earth.

God says that He *hates* a *"lying tongue"*. As a matter of fact Proverbs 12:22 says, *"Lying lips are an abomination to the Lord"*. The one sin that Jesus said would not be forgiven has to do with the use of man's tongue. Specifically, He says:

"Anyone who speaks a word against the Son of Man, it will be forgiven him; but whoever speaks against the Holy Spirit, it will not be forgiven him, either in this age or in the age to come".

Three of the seven things God says He hates have to do with man's use of his tongue. I believe, that when God created man, it was His intention that man would only say: (1) what God says and thinks, (2) that which he knows to be true, and (3) what he possesses within himself. This made his words powerful, reliable and indistinguishable from God's words. Therefore, nature and every created thing obeyed man as if God Himself was speaking to it. Man's words had authority because he possessed what he said and had no doubt concerning God's will and the truthfulness of his statements. This is why we are to fill our hearts and minds with the Word of God. When we do this, we can have confidence in what we say. Jesus said:

"A good man out of the good treasure of his heart brings forth good; and an evil man out of the evil treasure of his heart brings forth evil.

For out of the abundance of the heart his mouth speaks".[21]

This is why I believe that the most diabolical thing a man can do is lie. A lie uses the authority and power found in the law of the tongue, to be used for the purpose of establishing as truth something that is false. If the lie is not confronted with truth, it fortifies itself with the purpose of being accepted as truth. This untruth, once accepted as truth, becomes a law in the life of those under its influence. Due to the authority it has established in the lives of those under its influence, it causes them to live their lives in error as well as infecting others with the error.

I've often tried to imagine what nature did the first time it experienced man telling a lie. I believe that nature, because it was accustomed to man being a mouthpiece for God, became confused as to what it should do when man spoke something that wasn't true. Never before had creation experienced the other authorized speaking spirit

---

[21] Luke 6:45

saying something it did not believe, desire or intend to happen.

God created words as containers to carry substance from the intangible realm into the tangible realm. They are the common currency between the spiritual and physical realms of existence. They often outlive the life of the one who spoke them and eternally impact the life of the one who heard the words spoken. Words have assignments. Whenever, someone uses the occasion of speaking to create something that does not edify, God holds them accountable. This is because once spoken, the words cannot be retrieved but seek a place and opportunity to manifest themselves.

We must be careful in how we use the power that God has given us in speaking. Satan is always seeking a way to contaminate our hearts and minds so that what we speak will contaminate God's plan for our lives. Words can heal, break, destroy and save. Death and life are in the power of the tongue. We control whether or not God's Will or the enemy's will is done in the earth by what we allow to flow from our mouths. The Apostle Paul warned:

> *"Therefore, putting away lying, "Let each one of you speak truth with his neighbor"[22]*

The Power of Inspiration

In our look at Genesis 2:7, we discovered that the word used for *"breathed"* and *"breath"* literally meant to *"inspire"*. This inspiration was more than God causing man to become a living human being, but actually was an endowment and provision for man to exercise dominion in the earth. This endowment was mentioned in the definition given in the Merriam Webster dictionary for the word *inspired*. In reflecting on this definition, it specifically states that the word *inspire* means: *To influence, move or guide by divine or supernatural means; to communicate to an agent supernaturally: to draw forth or bring out thoughts.*[23]

---

[22] Ephesians 4:25

[23] Merriam-Webster's Online Dictionary - http://www.merriam-webster.com/dictionary/inspire

God gave man the ability, through supernatural (spiritual) means to be led, influenced and to even draw from His thoughts and words. These words do not originate in the mind of the person who speaks them, but from God Himself. This was God's intention from the very beginning.

Restoration of Inspiration

When man fell he lost the ability to commune with God's mind and discern His thoughts the way he previously could, because he was now spiritually dead.
Therefore, God had to write His will on tablets of stone and in the law of Moses until the time came where man again possessed the ability to have the mind of God. The Bible tells us that Jesus restored this ability to man through our faith in Him and rebirth as spiritual sons of God.

The Apostle Paul wrote the church at Rome and explained that a characteristic of someone who has been spiritually born again is their ability to be influenced and directed by the Spirit of God. Specifically, he wrote:

> *"For as many as are led by the Spirit of God, these are sons of God".*[24]

He goes further to explain to the church at Corinth that they now have access to God's mind through the Holy Spirit. Specifically, he wrote:

> *But as it is written: "Eye has not seen, nor ear heard, Nor have entered into the heart of man The things which God has prepared for those who love Him." But God has revealed them to us through His Spirit. For the Spirit searches all things, yes, the deep things of God. For what man knows the things of a man except the spirit of the man which is in him? Even so no one knows the things of God except the Spirit of God. Now we have received, not the spirit of the world, but the Spirit who is from God, that we might know the things that have been freely given to us by God. These things we also speak, not in words which man's wisdom teaches but which the Holy Spirit teaches, comparing spiritual things with spiritual. But the natural man does not receive the things of the Spirit of God, for they are foolishness to him; nor can he know them, because they are spiritually*

---

[24] Romans 8:14

46

discerned. But he who is spiritual judges all things, yet he himself is rightly judged by no one. For "who has known the mind of the Lord that he may instruct Him?" But we have the mind of Christ"[25]

Paul basically says that there are things that an unregenerated man will not be able to discern because he does not possess the Holy Spirit. However, when we are spiritually born again, we occupy the position that Adam occupied prior to the fall – spiritual sons of God. The same Holy Spirit that gave Adam access and understanding of God's thoughts and mind, we likewise have access to because we have the mind of Christ.

This inspiration or impartation from God restores our ability to experience the dominion that He decreed over man in the beginning. Without the ability to have access to God's mind, His thoughts and His words, we become subject to the situations that confront us in day to day life. God's creative but spiritual thoughts and Word require a means of impacting the physical world. God

---

[25] 2Corinthians 4:9-16

created us in His likeness, as another speaking spirit, to cause His will to be done on earth as it is in heaven. When we re-learn how to talk like God, and not as mere men, we will again realize the dominion God gave us from the very beginning.

The Law of Confession

Confession is a law. The true power in confession is found in our likeness to God and our ability to agree with and say what He has said. As mentioned previously, Genesis 1:26 reveals that God intended for man to have the ability to think and speak like Him. He specifically created us with the powerful ability to speak like He speaks. We are speaking spirits housed in earthen bodies for the purpose of administering and ruling an earthly kingdom for our heavenly King. As a matter of fact, we were created to say what God says and be His mouthpiece or representative in the earth.

To truly understand and appreciate the impact of this power we must once again, remove ourselves from thinking religiously. This is due to confession having taken on a meaning within the religious community that is contrary to its grammatical and true definition. AS a consequence, confession has lost its impact and importance in the lives of believers because we do not have a true understanding of what confession actually is.

Say That

"Confession Defined"

Biblically, confession has a drastically different meaning than understood by the vast majority of the religious community and institutions of the world. The word confession, as used in the New Testament, comes from the Greek word "*homologia*" which comes from the word "*homologeo*". Homologeo is comprised of two words. The first word is "*homo*" which means "*together*" or "*the same".* The second word is *"logos"* which means *"word".* Therefore, confession or "homologeo" literally means, *to "say the same thing" or "to speak together".* *Logos* root word *"lego"* carries with it the connotation of speaking with authority. Therefore, confession could be defined as: *Our ability and act of speaking in agreement with what God has said.* This is important and powerful in the life of the believer.

"Confession"

Satan, being our chief accuser, knows the power of confession. He has done everything he can to obscure and pervert our understanding of confession so that we never, with understanding, deploy its power against him and his kingdom. Satan has used religion and the world's system to cause believers to shy away from participating in true confession due to a lack of understanding of what confession truly is. When properly employed, confession empowers us to operate in the likeness of God causing us to have dominion in the earth and over the enemy. As such, we possess the power to undo and destroy the works of the enemy by decreeing and enforcing God's Word and rule in the earth and him. Having an understanding of confession is necessary in order for us to advance God's kingdom and realize the potential that God has placed within us.

The Law of Confession

It is important to understand, that confession is a law. Law, from a Kingdom perspective, is an authoritative enactment or decree issued by a king or governing power to accomplish a predetermined end. God's purpose in granting man His image was to enable him to exercise dominion in and over the earth. This would primarily be accomplished through man's ability to know God's thoughts and continually speaks God's words in and over the earth. As mentioned earlier, man's dominion over the earth would not be accomplished by his might or muscle, but by the authorized and purposeful use of his mouth. His ability to speak authoritatively and creatively as God does distinguishes and empowers man to have dominion over all the rest of creation.

Because confession is a law established by God to enable man to maintain dominion in the earth it can produce both the good and bad, based upon what man confesses or permits to come out of his mouth. *Cup it !*

In Genesis chapter 11, we witness the power inherent in man's ability to speak by him achieving that which seemed impossible simply by exercising his ability to speak. In Genesis 11, God declares that, unless He comes down and disrupts man's ability to speak and agree with one another, nothing they attempt would be impossible for him to do.[26] Just as these fallen men were able to employ the laws concerning agreement and speaking for wrong purposes or good. We can achieve anything by employing our words for the advancement of God's Kingdom. Our words, whether from God or some other

---

[26] Genesis 11:5-9

source, receive authorization to manifest in our lives when we speak them.

Remember, speaking is not simply making noise, but an act of authority. When we speak we are acting in the likeness of the One who acts by His Words. This is why Satan has worked so diligently to contaminate and corrupt our communication. By doing so, we give him place to manifest his will in the earth. Both God and Satan desire to use our mouth to manifest their will in our lives and in the earth. The Bible establishes that it is God's will that all men should come to a saving knowledge of His Son Jesus. However, we know that all men will not be saved. Those who are saved, accomplish this be engaging the Law of Confession. They come into agreement with and declare what God has already said concerning them. Specifically, the Bible says:

> *The word is near you, in your mouth and in your heart" (that is, the word of faith which we preach): that if you confess with your mouth the Lord Jesus and believe in your heart that God has raised Him from the dead, you will be saved. For with the heart one believes unto righteousness, and with the mouth confession is*

*made unto salvation. ... So then faith comes by
hearing, and hearing by the word of God".*[27]

Confession of God's word causes His will to manifest in
the life of the one speaking.

The Minds Mouth

The Law of Confession is so powerful because it is the
culmination of several laws that sustain God's order in
His Kingdom. The Law of Agreement, Creation and
Manifestation all are present when we engage the Law of
Confession. We must remember the definition of the
word confession, to understand how to properly operate
within the Law of Confession. Confession or "homologeo"
means, *to "say the same thing" or "to speak together"*. It
is as if God is the *mind* and we are the *mouth*. The
words that flow from our mouths are the very same
substance that exists in the mind of God.

---

[27] Romans 10:8-10, 17

mouth is simply the means of manifesting the things of the mind into the physical realm of existence. What was once confined to the intangible spiritual realm is now being expressed, revealed and declared in the physical realm of existence by words. It is the same mind and same word!

Ambassadors

After the fall of man, the Law of Confession enabled God to employ those who became citizens of His Kingdom, through faith in His Son Jesus Christ, to also become ambassadors for His Kingdom. The definition of confession given earlier contains the essence of the primary responsibility of an ambassador. An ambassador is only empowered to say what the king or his government authorizes him to say. He is not authorized to give his opinion or agree with anything contrary to the will of his king or government. He must say the same thing as the king. When an ambassador speaks, it is as if the king or the ambassador's government itself were speaking. He has the power to bind or forgive on behalf of his government. The ambassador and the kings words are the same. Every born again believer is an ambassador for the Kingdom of God.

The Apostle Paul stated this truth when he stated:

> *"Now then, we are ambassadors for Christ, as though God were pleading through us: we implore you on Christ's behalf, be reconciled to God."*[28]

Paul admonishes the people to receive his message as if God Himself were before them speaking. Paul's description of himself as ambassador indicated to his audience that he was not there on his own accord or in his own authority or power. His status as an ambassador communicated to his audience that: (1) his words were not his own, (2) he was authorized and empowered by the King, (3) there acceptance or rejection of his words were in essence an acceptance or rejection of the King's Words.

---

[28] 2Corinthians 5:20

Therefore, every time an ambassador of a kingdom speaks in his official capacity, he is observing the law of confession. This is how the believer is to operate in the world – confessing the Word of God everywhere and in every situation. We are to tell the world what *"thus saith the Lord"*, without fear of rejection. Jesus verified this fact when He told His disciples:

> *"He who hears you hears Me, he who rejects you rejects Me, and he who rejects Me rejects Him who sent Me"* [29].

This is the mentality we must have. The Law of Confession requires us to say what God says, without compromise. This applies not only to what we say to other people, but what we say to ourselves when we're faced with situations that are contrary to the will of God for our lives. Jesus spoke to a storm that tried to prevent His words from being fulfilled, after He declared that He and his disciples were going to the other side of the lake [30]. Jesus cursed a fig tree because it withheld from the Son of Man that which He had need of and had a

---

[29] Luke 10:16
[30] Mark 4:35-41

right to. Jesus spoke to what appeared to be insufficient provision after He decided that none should leave His presence hungry.

Confident confession is a consequence of knowing the will of God and having the conviction to say what God has said, even in the face of contradiction. The facts are one thing, but the truth of God's Word is another. The Word always prevails! Our job is to say what, *"thus saith the Lord!"*

An Ambassador's Privilege

It must be noted that an ambassador is one of the highest ranking officials a government or king can commission. Because of the great importance placed upon the ambassadors job he enjoy several privileges that are not granted other officers or citizens. To begin, ambassadors are generally exempt: (1) from having to pay personal debts, (2) taxes, (3) prosecution by foreign nation (except in rare cases), (4) being subject to the economic condition of the nation in which he is commissioned. An ambassador's quality of living is not determined by the condition of the host nation, but that of the nation from which he is sent. Although physically located in the host nation, his lodging and personal property is considered the sovereign territory and possession of his home nation. The embassy in which he lives is legally considered the sovereign property of his government.

This is the privilege that every believer enjoys as a consequence of their embracing their commission as an ambassador and authorized "confessor" on behalf of the Kingdom of God. As such, our quality of life is not determined by this world's system or the limitation that plague it. Jesus said that His Kingdom is not of or from this world, and promised if we sought it first that all that we need would be given to us.[31] This is the privilege of an ambassador. As long as an ambassador is faithful in his communication and confession of what his king or

---

[31] John 18:36, Matthew 6:33

government says, he is exempt from many of the burden borne by those who do not live by the Law of Confession.

Confession As a Profession

Having discovered the biblical definition for confession and realized the important role it plays in our ability to have dominion in the earth, it becomes clear that God created man to echo what He has said in heaven here in the earth. This ability and responsibility of man was the first official act God commanded man to do on behalf of the Kingdom. Shortly after forming man and all the animals of the earth, God brought them all before Adam to be named by him. God, when He created them knew what their names were, but needed Adam to be the one in the earth realm to speak their names because he (and man) were the ones given authority and jurisdiction over all that was in the earth. Adam, utilizing the access he had to God's mind simply gave the animals the names that God had already established when He created them. Adam did not make up names based on the first thing that crossed his mind. He was an ambassador, whose primary responsibility it was to say what the King and his government says. This was not a test of Adam's wit, but an official act in his capacity as an ambassador of the Kingdom in the earth. Adam repeated to God's physical creation what it's Creator had declared concerning them from His heavenly kingdom. As the authorized agent of the Kingdom in the earth, Adam observed the Law of Confession and was faithful in repeating what the King in heaven had said. Adam official duty as an ambassador was to confess what God had said concerning the matter. As a result, the Bible says that whatever Adam called the creature, "*that was its name* ".[32]

This official act of confession is an essential component of man's profession, as an ambassador, in the earth. Confession is the believer's job or profession. It gives us access to the things of God, and engenders within us confidence that whatever we says, we will have.

---

[32] Genesis 2:19

Religions Definition of Confession

Now that we understand what confession is from a biblical standpoint, I want to distinguish it from what has religiously become understood as confession by many.

In my life, I have been formally and informally, instructed in what constitutes *"confession"*, only to discover that this education was in error. As a result, I was unable to participate in the Law of Confession due to my understanding of what it meant to *confess* a thing. To illustrate this, let me share a personal side of my life that I believe will shed light on the source of much of the confusion many of us face concerning confession.

As a child, my parents removed me from the local public school I was attending due to the negative influences I encountered on a daily basis. Specifically, I had a propensity to fight over everything. As a result, at the end of my first grade year, it was highly suggested that I not return to the school and that my parents seek an environment that could offer me the discipline and structure I needed. That's right, I was expelled from school after the first grade. This should engender hope in as all of us. If God could use me, then He certainly can use anyone else, regardless of their pasts and histories.

As a result, I was enrolled in a Catholic school across town. The first day at my new school I became engaged in a verbal altercation, which quickly turned physical. In other words, I got into a fight my first day at my new school. As a consequence of this, I was assigned "homeroom" with one of the school's most notorious disciplinarian nuns. She kept a ruler at her desk, as well as a wooden cane that she used as she saw fit on any unruly kids. After years of being under this strict and discipline intensive environment, I learned how to control myself and get along with others.

While a student at this school, I served as an alter boy. Daily, I assisted the priest with preparing for mass while learning the religious traditions of the church. One tradition practiced by those who attended the school (and church) was the requirement of confession. Confession basically consisted of my telling the priest what I did wrong since my last confession. Once I told the priest all the sins I could remember, he would declare them forgiven and assign some form of penance to be performed for my being forgiven.

This religious understanding of confession shaped my perspective of what it meant to participate in confession. As a result, I associated confession with the commission of sin. Therefore, my experience taught me that confession was not a consequence of something good, but a fruit of wrongdoing. The more I confessed, the more I was reminded of how unworthy I was as a child of God.

While I benefited greatly from the discipline and self-control developed as a student at this Catholic school, it would take many years for me to overcome the misconception concerning the role confession played in my life as a believer.

"Higher Education"

This faulty understanding of confession was further fortified by my study of law. During my study in law school, we were taught that confession was an admission of guilt or an incriminating statement made by the accused.[33] More specifically, it is a statement made against one's own best interest. Again, confession was viewed in a negative light and the activity that a guilty party engaged in as a result of wrong having been committed. As a result, of being religious and professionally educated that confession was not a positive activity, I refrained from practicing it as a born again believer.

After reflecting on the religious and secular understanding of confession, it is clear that Satan has, in a large degree, succeeded in perverting our understanding of the power and truth found in confession. From a Kingdom perspective, confession is

---

[33] Barron's Law Dictionary, 3rd Edition, Steven H. Gifis.

what facilitates our salvation and manifestation of God's will in our lives. Without it, we become subject to situations and circumstances that are far below God's will for our lives. In order to regain dominion in our lives and advance God's Kingdom, we must rediscover the Law of the Tongue and the power of confession and use them to God's glory!

The Law of the Tongue

The Law of Binding and Loosing

In Matthew chapter 16, Jesus makes reference to another law given to the believer that is closely related to the Law of Confession. This law I will refer to as the "Law of Binding and Loosing". To properly understand this power, we must discuss it while keeping it within its proper context. The terms described as to "bind" and "loose" are found within the context of Jesus discussing the important role confession will play in the establishment of an earthly embassy or church.

The text in which this law is articulated is often misunderstood because of the religious interpretation given it. The text is found in the Gospel of Matthew, where Jesus asks His disciples who do men say that I am? After receiving several answers, Peter says something that Jesus uses as an opportunity to introduce and instruct the New Testament's leadership in the importance and power found in observing the Law of Confession. Specifically, the text reads:

> *"He said to them, "But who do you say that I am?" Simon Peter answered and said, "You are the Christ, the Son of the living God." Jesus answered and said to him, "Blessed are you, Simon Bar-Jonah, for flesh and blood has not revealed this to you, but My Father who is in heaven. And I also say to you that you are Peter, and on this rock I will build My church, and the gates of Hades shall not prevail against it. And I will give you the keys of the kingdom of heaven, and whatever you bind on earth will be bound in heaven, and whatever you loose on earth will be loosed in heaven".[34]*

To begin, Jesus declares that Peter is *"blessed"*. In order to maintain consistency in understanding throughout

---

[34] Matthew 16:15-19

this teaching series, whenever we use the term blessed, it will denote the bestowal of an *empowerment to succeed*. Blessing is a provision to be productive and to have success. Therefore, when Jesus declares that Peter is *blessed*, He is indicating that Peter is the recipient of an empowerment that will cause him to be productive and successful. What was the blessing and provision? It was Peter's ability to hear and repeat what he heard God say in heaven. Jesus, specifically said that Peter's revelation did not come from the earth realm. Peter received this insight, not as a consequence of formal education, but divine revelation from God. Jesus goes on to say, that upon *this rock*, which was Peter's ability to hear and confess with his mouth that which he heard declared by the word of God in heaven, will be the foundation in which the church (ecclesia) is built. The church's foundation is, not the person of Peter, but its ability to confess the Word of God.. This truth is verified in the Book of Romans, when Paul explains:

> *"But what does it say? "The word is near you, in your mouth and in your heart (that is, the word of faith which we preach): that if you confess*

with your mouth the Lord Jesus and believe in your heart that God has raised Him from the dead, you will be saved. For with the heart one believes unto righteousness, and with the mouth confession is made unto salvation".[35]

Romans 10:17 explains that this word of faith, which has found its way into the mouth of the one making confession, did so through the hearing of what God has said. Therefore, this person heard God say something, which they believed and agreed with, which caused what they heard to manifest in their lives by their confession of it.

Therefore, the act and Law of Confession is an essential element of the New Testament believer's born again experience. Without it, salvation could not manifest in their life.

---

[35] Romans 10:8-10

The Power of Binding and Loosing

The words of Jesus as it pertains to our confession cannot be overlooked or underestimated in its impact on the quality of life we live here on earth. Jesus reveals that our ability to discern and repeat what God says in heaven gives us access to God's will manifesting in our lives here on earth.

Jesus grants this access to heaven by giving the believer what is described as *keys"*. It will become evident that these *keys* are really the Law of Confession being employed with understanding by a believer. By reading Matthew 16:19 from the Amplified translation of the Bible, the presence and operation of the Law of Confession is clearly seen as it relates to the Law of Binding and Loosing. Specifically, the text reads:

> *"I will give you the keys of the kingdom of heaven; and whatever you bind (declare to be improper and unlawful) on earth must be what is already bound in heaven; and whatever you loose (declare lawful) on earth must be what is already loosed in heaven" (Amplified).*

After Peter's confession (his having said what he heard God say), Jesus declares, as a consequence of this confession) keys have been given to him. These keys represent our access and authorization to things of God's heavenly kingdom, which can only be obtained through our confession of them. Our confession constitutes our possession of these things.

Confession provided access to the Kingdom, both for eternal salvation and temporal provision. Our access to these things in the heavenly Kingdom are qualified in the Amplified translation as being confined to that which is "already" bound or loosed in heaven. We cannot declare a thing so in the earth if it has not been likewise been declared so in heaven. There must be agreement on earth with what has *already* been established in heaven for us to have confidence of it manifesting in the earth. This is the Law of Binding and Loosing.

Again, confession is our saying what God has said. It is our agreeing in word with what God has declared.

Therefore, it violates the underlying principles and laws that support the operation of the Kingdom for us to declare something bound or loose that has not "already" been bound or loosed in heaven. The words "bind" and "loose" are actually referring to a things *legal standing* in the Kingdom. If something is prohibited from existing in God's Kingdom, we have the right to prohibit declare and declare it unlawful here in His earthly Kingdom.

Jesus said that the believer can invoke the Law of Binding and Loosing to change an earthly situation, if the situation has been declared unlawful in God's heavenly Kingdom. Remember, that both God's heavenly and earthly Kingdoms operate upon the basis of God's Word, which is its law. As an ambassador and citizen of the Kingdom, your quality of life is not determined by the condition of the territory you've been assigned, but by the home country's quality of living.

Therefore, if a believer finds themselves living beneath that which God has decreed as acceptable, they must employ the Law of Binding and Loosing to correct the *illegal or prohibited condition.* This is why it is critical to know the Word of God and develop a discernment and sensitivity to the move and voice of the Holy Spirit, so that you can be led in your speaking God's will into your situation.

"Must Already Be..."

I have heard many teach and preach that: "*Whatever you bind on earth will be bound in heaven, and whatever you loose on earth will be loosed in heaven.*" This assertion violates the law of confession. Confession requires us to get the substance of our confession from what has already been declared so in heaven, which we in turn reiterate and confirm as so in the earth – not vise versa. The effectiveness of our confession comes from the fact that what we confess is already a reality and in existence. We are asking for anything to be created, but to manifest in the earth as it is already established in God's heavenly kingdom. Therefore, we are simply informing the natural world of the true state of things, prior to their manifesting physically in it.

In it simplest form, confession is the revelation of God's will in the earth via our agreement in word. Our grant access to heavenly realities enables us to establish what has been revealed to us here in the earth. This is why, Jesus taught the disciples to pray that: *God's Kingdom come and will be done on earth as it "already" is being done in heaven[36]*. God intends that we cultivate and seed the earth with His Word and will until heaven's culture manifests itself here in the earth.

In pondering a way to best communicate the laws, principles, concepts and truths that under-gird the related Laws of the Tongue, I've decided to use an analogy that likens confession to how a bank account operates.

---

[36] Matthew 6:10

When I get paid I never see the money I receive from my work because it is electronically deposited into my bank account without me having to physically handle my check or the money. I am made aware of the deposit because the "source" of the funds promised to pay me a certain amount of money on a certain day of the month. When I need cash I go to an ATM that operates on the same system that my bank operates and make a demand for money that I've never personally handled but have the revelation of its reality and availability in my account. My demand is a reflection of my conviction of the sources ability to provide what is promised and my understanding that it is available to me now, despite the fact that I've never personally handled or seen the cash. The only thing the ATM can manifest is what *already* exists in the account. I cannot command the ATM to produce something that did not already exist. The source must have already declared and released the substance of what I am make a demand on for there to be a legitimate expectation of manifestation.

The ATM functions much like the words of our confession. When we confess a matter as so in the earth, we are really responding to the revelation that it is so in heaven and ordained by God. Our words make a withdrawal from *The Source* of all things (the Word of God) which cannot be seen and brings the substance of this Word into our temporal and tangible world. To go to an ATM and make a demand for cash without personally having made a deposit, or having been informed that such deposit was made by another source, would not be faith at all but an act of futility – even foolishness. Why? Because the substance upon which you are making a demand does not exist. *When !*

Many people who approach confession from this perspective believe that a naked *desire or hope* for a thing establishes it as so. They speak words based on this hope hoping that what they say will manifest. They bind and loose thing only to discover that the situation has not changed. This is because it violates the Law of Confession. The Law of Confession requires that what we confess we also possess. We must get the substance for our confession from the Source of all things – God and His Word[37]. The Amplified Bible's translation of Matthew 16:19 articulates this law concisely when it says:

> *"I will give you the keys of the kingdom of heaven; and whatever you bind (declare to be improper and unlawful) on earth must be what is already bound in heaven; and whatever you loose (declare lawful) on earth must be what is already loosed in heaven."*

The *perfect passive participle* found within this text indicates that what is forbidden or permitted was already in existence prior to it being forbidden or permitted in the earth.

Therefore, when we speak, we are not hoping something will happen. We are literally making a demand upon and withdrawal of realities that are already in existence. This is why we can have confidence in it manifesting in the earth. Confession is not an act of creation, but manifestation. Our words are the vehicle by which that

---

[37] Genesis chapter 1, John 1:1-4, Colossians 1:16-17,Hebrews 11:3

which already exist is transported and introduced into another realm existence. The intangible word (the substance of all things) is spoken and communicated into a tangible world where it will find expression and manifestation. This is the Law of Confession.

The Law of Binding and Loosing

The law concerning binding and loosing in the Kingdom is not strictly a New Testament law. This law was actually introduced to us in the Old Testament. Specifically, it concerned vows or oaths taken by a man or woman to do or not to do a thing. Their oaths and vows were believe to have the power to "bind" or "loose" their souls in a matter. God instructed Moses in the Book of Numbers to educate the people of the power and impact their words had on their lives. Their understanding of the power of their words had been lost during their 400 years in Egyptian bondage. They had become careless with their words and placed little significance upon the impact they had, not only on their physical existence but, on their souls as well. Specifically, Moses instructed the people:

> *"If a man makes a vow to the Lord, or swears an oath to bind himself by some agreement, he shall not break his word; he shall do according to all that proceeds out of his mouth.'*... 'Or if a woman makes a vow to the Lord, and binds herself by some agreement' .... 'If indeed she takes a husband, while bound by her vows or by a rash utterance from her lips by which she bound herself, and her husband hears it, and makes no response to her on the day that he hears, then her vows shall stand, and her agreements by which she bound herself shall stand. But if her husband overrules her on the day that he hears it, he shall make void her vow which she took and what she uttered with her lips, by which she bound herself, and the Lord will release her. [38]

This text makes clear that God honors our words, whether they are for our good or bad. We establish what will and will not enter into our lives by what we commit ourselves to via our words. As mentioned earlier, confession is how we are saved. We confess our faith in Christ, and Christ becomes

---

[38] Numbers 30:2, 6-8

a reality in our lives. Something spiritual transpires as a result of our words. Our words are the authorized and established means by which we interact and transact with the spiritual realm. Words are the common currency in both the spirit and natural realms of existence.

This principle was reiterated and reinforced by Jesus in the New Testament when Jesus said that we have legal access to those things in God's heavenly Kingdom by our binding and loosing them in our lives here on the earth.

This Law of Binding and Loosing is a God given ability that empowers us to fulfill our mandate of dominion and to facilitate His will being done on earth, as it is in heaven!

The Law of the Tongue

The Power of Life and Death

"A man's stomach shall be satisfied from the fruit of his mouth, from the produce of his lips he shall be filled. Death and life are in the power of the tongue, And those who love it will eat its fruit."
Proverbs 18:20-21

As we have already discovered, our ability to speak is a consequence of our likeness to God. God in creating rulers for His physical Kingdom, created beings that not only resembled Him in their image, but had the ability to "act" like Him. Whenever God wanted to *do* something He *said* something. As a result, whatever He *said* ultimately became *seen*. God's speaking was the act. God established the order by which the world operates by speaking to it. When God wanted to give life to something, He spoke to it. When He decided to create man, He spoke him into existence.[39] Then God formed man from the dust of the ground and breathed into him the *breadth of life*, causing the spirit man to become a living soul or human being[40]. This new creation was a trinity (just like God) who had the ability to act like God. Just as God is Father, Son and Holy Spirit, the *human being* is mind, body and spirit. This was the ruler God gave dominion to.

Man's first official act as ruler of the earth was to speak to its inhabitants because speaking is an act

---

[39] Genesis 1:26
[40] Genesis 2:7

or exercise of authority! When we speak we arrest
and put in motion spiritual realities whose purpose
it is to carryout and manifest what it is we've said.
This is why it is so important that we view our
words as substance. They are the building blocks
upon which our lives are built and shaped. If we
want life, we must first possess and then speak it.
God honors our words, and so should we.

Speaking Life

I've heard it said that: *"Whatever you speak to you
give life to".* This is actually a *law* within the
Kingdom of God! It has been scientifically proven
that people who have plants speak to them
regularly, they live longer. For that matter, it is
also scientifically proven, that the elderly who have
regular conversation with others live longer. Any
relationship with open lines of communication, last

longer. Businesses with good internal communication do better than those businesses that do not. Why is this? It is a law by which God ordered the world and His Kingdom. This law is so powerful, that God used it against man to frustrate their plans to build a monument unto themselves.

Babel

Earlier in our study on the Law of the Tongue, we observed in Genesis chapter 11 that man used his ability to communicate and agree with one another to do what could be considered an impossibility at that time. Genesis 11 records that man settled in the plain of Shinar and decided to build a city and a tower whose top would pierce the floor of heaven.[41] In utilizing their likeness to God by creatively imagining something that never existed before, and

---

[41] Genesis 11:4

through their ability to communicate with one another, they began to do what seemed impossible. God taking note of this said:

> *"Indeed the people are one and they all have one language, and this is what they begin to do; now nothing that they propose to do will be withheld from them."*[42]

God testifies that their ability to speak to one another was the foundation of their success. God says nothing about their physical strength or their numbers but points to their tongue as being the thing that was empowering them. This fact is seen in how God decides to stop their building project. The Bible records that God said:

> *"Come, let Us go down and there confuse their language, that they may not understand one another's speech." So the Lord scattered them abroad from there over the face of all the earth, and they ceased building the city.*[43]

---

[42] Genesis 11:6
[43] Genesis 11:7-8

God did not stop their building project with a
tornado, angel or disease, but by impacting their
ability to speak and communicate with one another.
By impacting their ability to talk to one another,
God interrupted the lifeline of the project thereby
causing it to die immediately.

The Tower of Babel demonstrates that man
operating by a law that had not been repealed as a
result of the fall. The Law of the Tongue is effective
whether employed for good or evil purposes. Your
words will give life to and manifest what you say.
They posses the substance of what is in your heart
and can be transferred to the hearer for their
possession. The Tower of Babel started in the mind
of people's leaders, who told someone else, who
received what they said and told someone else and
so on. The tongue was used to take the substance
that their leaders possessed to pass onto others who
originally had no idea a tower was possible. Once

they had heard and received what was said, it became a reality in their lives as well.

It is interesting to note that God used this same power in the New Testament to establish, unify and men in establishing His church. The event is recorded in Act 2 where it reads:

> *"When the Day of Pentecost had fully come, they were all with one accord* in one place. And suddenly there came a sound from heaven, as of a rushing mighty wind, and it filled the whole house where they were sitting. Then there appeared to them divided tongues, as of fire, and one sat upon each of them. And they were all filled with the Holy Spirit and began to speak with other tongues, as the Spirit gave them utterance. And there were dwelling in Jerusalem Jews, devout men, from every nation under heaven. And when this sound occurred, the multitude came together, and were confused, because everyone heard them speak in his own language.*[44]

In this instance, the word *tongue* means *"languages"*. God removed the effects that the Tower of Babel had in

---

[44] Acts 2:1-6

scattering mankind, due to the inability to communicate with one another, by empowering everyone to understand what was being said in their own language. Mankind, for this moment and purpose, was again one in the earth in their language. Due to God employing the Law of the Tongue on Pentecost, over 3000 souls were born again and added to His Kingdom. In this instance, the tongue was the facilitator of new life!

Imparting Life

Jesus certainly understood the power of the tongue and its ability to impart life. Jesus used His tongue to restore what God originally gave man in the Garden and to take authority over that which was contrary to God's Will for man.

In the garden, prior to man's fall, God established an environment that reflected His Will for mankind. There was no death, sickness, insufficiency, infirmity, demon possession or life-threatening storm. Therefore, we witness Jesus, throughout the gospels continually addressing these manifestations by speaking to them. By speaking to them, He released what He had on the inside of Him. In some instances it was healing, while in others it was deliverance, in one form or another.

The power of the tongue was never so evident as when it was used to overcome death. The Gospel of John records that Jesus' close friend Lazarus died and had been in the grave for 4 days.[45] Jesus had previously received news that Lazarus was sick and was being beckoned to come and heal him. Jesus waited until Lazarus was dead to begin His journey to his house. Upon His arrival everyone thought that it was too late to raise him from the dead due to a Jewish myth that the spirit of the deceased remained around the body for 3 days. This being the forth day, they were certain that death would prevail. Even when Jesus told them what He would do, they did not believe. Jesus was taken to the place where

---

[45] John 11:1-44

Lazarus was laid and gave orders that the entrance of the tomb be cleared of its stone. He stood at a distance and does something amazing. Jesus does not go into the tomb or request that those who rolled away the stone bring him Lazarus out. Jesus spoke with a loud and commanding voice: *"Lazarus, come forth!"*

Jesus sent life, via His words, on an assignment into the realms of the dead, to bring Lazarus back alive. Jesus was careful to specify whom He was calling or else risk every grave within the sound of His voice obeying Him and releasing its occupant. Lazarus came forth bound in His grave close - alive! No hands were laid on him, only the word of life had been spoken. Jesus utilized the Law of the Tongue to reach into realms that His physical body could not go. God testifies of this law when He speaks of His words having an assignment. Specifically, He said:

> *"So shall My word be that goes forth from My mouth; It shall not return to Me void, But it shall accomplish what I please, And it shall prosper in the thing for which I sent it."*[46]

---

[46] Isaiah 55:11

Our words, like God's words, are alive and have an assignment when spoken. Because we are created in God's likeness, we have the power to speak life and cause it to manifest in our situations. Many people do not experience the manifestation of what they say because they violate a related law that requires them to possess what they say or confess. When we speak without possessing what we say, these are empty words and have no substance to impact our situation with. This principle is inherent in every law that concerns the act of speaking. Effective and authoritative speech is a consequence of making a withdrawal of what one already possesses in their heart by means of their words. Their mouths and words are simply a medium of communicating and transporting into the tangible world, that which one possesses in their intangible being.

The reason Jesus could confidently declare life in the face of death was because He was life. Jesus not only possessed resurrection power – He was the power of resurrection! He boldly declared: *"I am the resurrection and the life[47],* and in another place, *""I am the way, the truth, and the life.[48]* He possessed the power of life on the inside of Him. His tongue and words were simply the medium by which He delivered life to those in need of it.

This is why what we listen to and say will determine what we receive in life. What we hear from the mouth of others will take root within us and ultimately become our words and manifest in our lives.

Speaking Death

Several years ago I was watching a Christian ministries' television program who ministers to an Indian tribe in plains area of the United States. This tribe, having learned English, refused to speak it because they considered English the *"language of death"*. This caught my attention.

---

[47] John 11:25a
[48] John 14:16

A representative of this tribe went on to explain that when English speaking people come to visit and minister to them they often talk about sickness, tragedy and other forms of mishap in their everyday conversation - even in the presence of those who are sick. They found this to be very disturbing because they believe that their words possessed the power to cause what is spoken to actually come to pass. Therefore, if a person were sick, you would not speak of them being sick or talk about their condition worsening or them dying. They consider this the equivalent of someone cursing them. You would instead speak about their getting better and the life they have ahead of them. This Native American tribe had become Christian, but decided to hold onto a truth that much of the church has forgotten or overlooked. Our words have power and determine the various outcomes we experience in our lives.

"Say What You Mean"

The enemy has incorporated into our everyday language terminology and words that are contrary to their actual meaning. Let me provide a couple examples of words that are commonly used but have significantly different meanings than their everyday usage. In our society today, the word *"incredible"* is used to describe something outstanding. However the word literally means: *that which is not trustworthy* or *worthy of being believed.* WHAT! I've had people approach me after delivering a sermon and say: *"Pastor that was incredible"*. I knew what they meant to say, but that wasn't what they actually said. They literally said that what I preached was not trustworthy or worthy of being believed. That's quite a difference between what *was meant to be said* and what *was actually said.*

Another word that is in common use today, but has a significantly different meaning than how it is used today is the word *"mortgage"*. I've heard countless people declare that they are seeking a mortgage for their homes. The word *mortgage* is made up of two words "mort" and "gage". The first word that comprises the word mortgage is the word *"mort"* means *"death"*. The second word in the word mortgage is the word *"gage"* means *"grip"*.

Therefore, the word mortgage literally means "death grip". Financial institutions around the world daily offer people mortgages with 15 and 30 years terms. I don't know about you, but I don't want any form of a *death grip* in my life, not even for a single day, and certainly not for 15 or 30 years..

Finally, there is the word *"religion"*. The word *religion* is comprised of the prefix *"re"* and the word *"ligion"*. The prefix *"re"* means *"to do again"* or *"go back to"*. The word *"ligion"* means *"constraint"*. Its root word is the same word from which we get the word *"ligature"*, which means to *bind, or to become tied or bound by*. Therefore, the word religion can literally be interpreted to means *"to become bound again"*. The Sadducees and Pharisees of Jesus' day exemplify this meaning of religion in scripture. Many today believe that religion will set them free, when its literal meaning says otherwise.

Granting Access

As mentioned previously, the act of speaking is one that must be approached responsibly. When we speak we are committing an act of natural and spiritual significance. We are either creating or destroying, giving life or death with our words.

In order for certain things to take place in the earth, God must rely on man to manifest and permit them. This law is seen throughout scripture when His prophets would speak to the people on God's behalf. The prophet would declare to the people, *"Thus saith the Lord ...."* so that they understood that it was not the man speaking, but God Himself through the man. God needs man's body, mind, mouth and will to manifest His will in the earth.

Therefore, it is clear that man is the gatekeeper as to whether or not a thing is realized in the earth. The gate, which both God and Satan seek control of, is man's mouth. This is why David said:

"Set a guard, O Lord, over my mouth; Keep watch over the door of my lips."[49]

David recognized that what came out his mouth not only had the ability to impact the lives of others, but their future generations as well.

Human beings, being the authorized medium of manifestation in the earth, grants the spiritual realities access into the physical world by they words. This is why Satan tries so diligently to control what we think, by flooding our eyes, ears and senses with his ways and thoughts, because he knows, if he can control or influence what a person thinks, he also can control what comes out of their mouths. What we allow in our eyes and ears becomes what we meditate on, which then becomes our thoughts. These established thoughts take root in our hearts. Once it takes root in our hearts, it is just a matter of time before it becomes the substance of our words. Jesus said:

---

[49] Psalms 141:3

"A good man out of the good treasure of his heart brings forth good; and an evil man out of the evil treasure of his heart brings forth evil. For out of the abundance of the heart his mouth speaks."[50]

This is precisely the reason it has become a habit for people to use words that are inherently harmful to express ideas that are contrary to what they actually mean or want to say. These exaggerations of words may seem harmless to the unsuspecting speaker, but are of the utmost importance to spiritual realities seeking an entrance and means of manifestation into the physical world.

I've heard people say things such as:

> *" I'd die for one of those".*
> *"My feet are killing me".*
> *"That drives me crazy."*
> *"I'm starving ... "*
> *"That's eating me up on the inside."*

---

[50] Luke 6:45

These kinds of statements may seem innocent to the speaker, however spiritual realities honor what we say and take them seriously and literally. God alone has the ability to search your heart and discern what you truly meant to say. However, every other created beings do not share the benefit of being omniscient and therefore must take our words as stated. If you jokingly declare that you are "sick to death" concerning a matter, you have provided the authorization and substance for an attending spirit to manifest your words in your life.

The only limitation placed upon the words we speak is whether or not we possess authority over the matter in which we've spoken. Remember, that God gave man authority over matters that pertain to the earth. Therefore, careless words concerning matter within the earth realm give the enemy the authorization to facilitate and implement their manifestation.

An example of this law at work can be found in the book of Genesis chapter 31, when Jacob fled from his uncle Laban in the middle of the night taking Laban's daughters (which were also Jacob's wives) and all he owned. When Laban caught up with Jacob, he asked Jacob why he left in the middle of the night, taking with him his property – namely his household idols or gods. Jacob vehemently denied this claim and declared that if anyone in his caravan took Laban's gods that they shall die[51]. Jacob's wife Rachel, who he worked 14 years to marry, was the one who took the gods. Laban never found the idols because Rachel lied and did not allow him to search her because she claimed to be menstruating. However, the words of Jacob had been spoken and the one he loved most shortly thereafter died giving birth to his son. Jacob never would have said anything that he thought would bring harm to the one he loved and worked 14 years to marry. However, when he careless spoke words authorizing the death of the one who took the idols, the enemy used his authority and words to quickly set about to bring his words to pass.

---

[51] Genesis 31:19-33

As mentioned earlier, we've been given power and authority in the earth concerning the affairs of men. We have the power to declare a matter and establish it with our words. We have the ability to impact both spiritual and physical realities with our words. We can bind and loose things that are so in heaven here on earth with our words. Due to our being created in the likeness of God, we too have the authority to bless and curse a thing with our words. Our words possess the power of life and death, blessing and cursing, just like God's words.

The Law of the Tongue

The Law of the Blessing and the Curse

The Blessing

In the book of Genesis we are introduced to spiritual forces that were initiated by God that impact our satisfaction and fulfillment in life today. These spiritual forces are known as the *blessing* and the *curse*.

Specifically, throughout the first chapter of Genesis we see God bestowing His "blessing" upon the fish of the sea and the birds of the air. The very first instance we hear

God blessing anything within His physical Kingdom was in Genesis 1:21-22 were it reads:

> *"So God created great sea creatures and every living thing that moves, with which the waters abounded, according to their kind, and every winged bird according to its kind. And God saw that it was good. And God blessed them, saying, "Be fruitful and multiply, and fill the waters in the seas, and let birds multiply on the earth."*

Again, in Genesis 1:27-28 we find this same language as it applies to man. Specifically, it reads:

> *"So God created man in His own image; in the image of God He created him; male and female He created them. Then God blessed them, and God said to them, "Be fruitful and multiply; fill the earth and subdue it; have dominion over the fish of the sea, over the birds of the air, and over every living thing that moves on the earth."*

In each case, the blessing was given *prior to* the command to be fruitful and multiply. God's issuance of the blessing prior to the commandment to be *fruitful and multiply* is and indication that our ability to be fruitful and experience increase in life is dependant upon the empowerment and presence of the blessing.

108

The Nature of the Blessing

The blessing, in its truest sense is a declaration of destiny and prosperity, as well as, an authorization and empowerment to succeed in the matter in which it is bestowed. It is an endowment of authority by God to overcome one's circumstances and to fulfill a predetermined purpose. It is spiritual in its origin with the purpose of impacting the natural world. Therefore, the "blessing" can be defined as a *"spoken spiritual impartation and empowerment to succeed, increase and prosper in order to fulfill a predetermined purpose or destiny"*.

The blessing is a spoken spiritual empowerment and endowment that is communicated and enacted by words. Our ability and empowerment of bestowing blessing is a consequence of our bearing the likeness of God. It is another provision of God for mankind to "have dominion" in the earth.

Having What You Say

The blessing is initiated not only by the words of the speaker, but by the speaker actual possession of what he or she says. In other words, the one bestowing the blessing must possess what they are trying to impart to the one being blessed. One cannot give what they themselves do not possess. This is a spiritual law that must be remembered. *You can only give what you possess.*

This law is clearly demonstrated in the life of the brothers Jacob and Esau. In Genesis chapter 27 were are told that Isaac, the father of Jacob and Esau, instructed Esau to catch some game so that he could prepare him his favor stew and afterwards bless him. Isaac's wife Rebekah overheard Isaac's plan to bless Esau and devised a plan by which Jacob, her favorite son, would receive Esau's blessing before he could return from hunting. Jacob followed his mother's instructions and received the blessing Isaac had reserved for Esau. Upon Esau's return from hunting and preparing his father's stew, he discovered that Jacob had tricked Isaac and taken the blessing. The Bible records that Esau pleaded with his father, saying:

> *"Have you not reserved a blessing for me?" Then Isaac answered and said to Esau, "Indeed I have made him your master, and all his brethren I have given to him as servants; with grain and wine I have sustained him. What shall I do now for you, my son?" And Esau said to his father, "Have you only one blessing, my father? Bless me--me also, O my father!" And Esau lifted up his voice and wept."[52]*

Isaac had already transferred the blessing he possessed upon Jacob and had nothing of the same caliber and substance left to give Esau. Therefore, he gave Esau what was left. Specifically, the Bible says:

> *"Then Isaac his father answered and said to him: "Behold, your dwelling shall be of the fatness of the earth, And of the dew of heaven from above. By your sword you shall live, And you shall serve your brother; And it shall come to pass, when you become restless, That you shall break his yoke from your neck."[53]*

---

[52] Genesis 27:36-38
[53] Genesis 27:39-40

111

This pronouncement of destiny was far from the blessing bestowed upon Jacob. This was not a consequence of the Isaac's will for his eldest son, but a matter of law. He had nothing left to give Esau in the form of a blessing. Once the blessing left his father's lips and the words were communicated to Jacob, they became the possession of Jacob. Isaac's words bound him to honor the blessing bestowed upon Jacob and established Jacob as the rightful owner of what was delivered to him by his father's words.

This law is critical to understand by those seeking a certain level of manifestation in their lives. You cannot receive a certain level of blessing from someone that does not possess the level of blessing being sought. From a natural standpoint, you would not ask or expect a homeless man to provide you with finances or a home. Why? Because he does not possess what you need. He cannot give you what he himself does not possess.

The same is true when dealing with spiritual matters and matters concerning the anointing. There are many men and women of God who have become stuck in relationships and allegiances with people who do not possess the anointing or blessing to empower them to occupy the place where God is calling them. Anything God will do in the earth, He will use a human being to do it. Therefore, if God wants to bless you, He will use someone who He has given the anointing and means to bless you.

Oftentimes, God will make it clear that He is directing an individual to a certain place and that person will refuse to go because they are afraid to leave that which has become comfortable and familiar. However, they soon become frustrated because they are not able to progress to the level of their gifting because there is no one in their circle or community who can pour into them what is necessary to go to the next level in which they are being called. The local leadership will pray and speak thing over this individual, but their words are of no effect because they do not possess what it is they are trying to bestow upon this person. This is the reason why God was leading the individual in another direction in order

to bring them into contact with the anointing necessary
for the person's destiny.

Super and Natural

It must be noted that the purpose in which blessings are
bestowed or given is to impact the individual's life and
circumstance *here on earth.* So many believers believe
that if the Bible mentions the word blessing it is confined
to the spiritual life of the person. This is not supported
by scripture. The Bible testifies that whenever God
blessed someone, they became fruitful and multiplication
took place in their lives. I have yet to find anyone that
God blessed and their circumstances worsened.

It has been argued that Jesus was blessed but yet end up
losing everything He owned – including His life.
However, when making this statement we must
remember His purpose in coming and what we qualify as
loss. Through His sacrifice He gained power over death,

hell and the grave and was given a name above every name and received all power in heaven and earth.

It must be remembered that every true blessing has the assignment of assisting in the manifestation of God predetermined purpose. It cannot be overlooked or underestimated that the blessing's purpose is to impact our circumstance as we live our natural lives in the earth. The blessing is a supernatural empowerment for our lives in our here and now.

Ephesians 1:3 declares:

> *"Blessed be the God and Father of our Lord Jesus Christ, who has blessed us with every spiritual blessing in the heavenly places in Christ,"*

All blessings, at their origin, are spiritual. The blessing itself cannot be seen however its presence can be seen. The blessing purpose is to manifest in the seen. Just as the wind itself cannot be seen, the impact of its presences can be seen.

The "spiritual blessing" described in Ephesians chapter one have their origin in the spiritual realm, not the earth. Therefore, they are reserved for us in heavenly places. Just as we saw earlier with Isaac's blessing of Jacob, God had already preordained and foreknew that Jacob would receive the blessing. Isaac's speech simply lined up with what had already been declared lawful in heaven and was released in the earth by his declaration of the same. This same pattern was followed in Matthew chapter 16 when Jesus declared that Peter's revelation and confession did not have its origins in the earth, but in heaven. Then Jesus proceeds to declare that whatever we bind on earth must be what is already bound in heaven, and whatever is loose or declare lawful on earth, must be what is already loosed or declared lawful in heaven. In essence, the things or blessings that have been declared lawful in heaven are reserved for those who discern their availability and God's will for them to be resident in the natural realm here in the earth.

Therefore, if God says that I'm blessed, I too can declare the same with confidence that it will become resident in my life. The blessing is not for heaven, but for our time here on earth. There are no needs in heaven. You can have no greater blessing than the very presence of God. You won't need an empowerment to succeed or overcome obstacles because they don't exist in heaven! The blessing's purpose is to facilitate increase, multiplication and prosperity in the life of the one being blessed in order to fulfill their God given purposes.

When God allowed man to hear Him declare a blessing over man, He at the same time authorized him to do the same thing. It is a law within the Kingdom that; *Whenever God allows man to see or hear Him do a thing that He at the same time authorizes man to do the same in the earth.* Because God allowed man to witness Him issuing a blessing, He likewise empowered and authorized man to do the same to others. Similarly, when man observed God issue a curse, man became empowered and authorized to do the same. The law is still active today in that, even after the fall of man he retained the ability to issue both blessings and curses.

The Curse

In the book of Genesis, we are introduced to the reality of there being such a thing as a curse. Within the first 4 chapters of Genesis, the Bible records 3 separate instances where God issues a curse. In Genesis chapter 3 we witness God cursing the serpent, then the ground. Because the serpent was used by Satan to cause the fall of mankind, God says to the serpent:

> *"Because you have done this, You are cursed more than all cattle, And more than every beast of the field."* [54]

The consequence of the serpent being cursed seemed to impact it's position within the animal kingdom (it being demoted) and its life being greatly complicated by it being required to move about without legs.

---

[54] Genesis 3:14

The second mention of a curse being issued is found in Genesis chapter 3 where God says to the ground:

> *"Cursed is the ground for your sake; In toil you shall eat of it All the days of your life. Both thorns and thistles it shall bring forth for you, And you shall eat the herb of the field. In the sweat of your face you shall eat bread Till you return to the ground, For out of it you were taken; For dust you are, And to dust you shall return."[55]*

Again, the curse complicates and impacts the ability of the thing being cursed to fulfill its created purpose. The curse spoken over the ground caused it to experience difficulty in doing what it was created to do – that is to provide for man.

Also, in Chapter 4 of Genesis, God issues another curse when speaking to Cain. Specifically, He said to Cain:

> *"What have you done? The voice of your brother's blood cries out to Me from the ground. So now you are cursed from the earth, which has opened its mouth to receive your brother's blood from your hand. When you till the ground, it shall no longer yield its strength*

---

[55] Genesis 3:17-19

*to you. A fugitive and a vagabond you shall be
on the earth.* [56]

Cain was subject to the previous curse on the ground, which required him toil and labor for his needs to be met. However, with this second cursing of the ground, God commands the earth to produce nothing at all for Cain. The impact of this curse was that the ground would produce nothing, even if Cain invested toil and labor.

There are some common and consistent characteristics of the curses issued in the Book of Genesis by God that can provide us understanding of what a curse truly is. In every case the object cursed: (1) had its created purpose frustrated, and (2) it ability to be fruitful was either complicated or completely hindered.

In summary, when God cursed the snake He confined its movement to crawling on its belly instead of walking about on legs. God did not kill the snake, but made its life more difficult. When God cursed the ground He

---

[56] Genesis 4:10-12

restrained it from yielding its increase to man until man made an investment of toil and labor. God did not prevent the ground from giving man what he needed, but made it substantially more difficult for him to receive what he needs. Finally, God commands the earth not to produce anything for Cain, even if he works the land. God did not kill Cain, but made it impossible for him to receive what he used to receive from the ground. Prior to this curse, Cain, like everyone else, had to toil and labor for the ground to give him anything. Now, the ground is prohibited from giving him anything, regardless of what he does to earn it.

In each case in which the curse was issued: (1) the curse is bestowed by the speaking of words, (2) the curse is spoken by One possessing the authority and power to enforce the curse, (3) the curse's origin is spiritual, (4) it directly impacts the quality of life of is recipient, (5) its purpose is to impact the natural or physical world, (6) the curse is a consequence of the violation of God's law, and (7) its primary objective is to frustrate the ability of its recipient to be productive and fulfill its creative purpose. Therefore, the *"curse"* can be defined as a:

> Spoken *spiritual impartation and empowerment to fail, serving to frustrate and complicate the fulfillment of one's creative purpose and destiny.*

In review of these characteristics, it is evident that the curse is the *opposite* of the blessing. As previously mentioned, the *"blessing"* is a:

> *Spoken spiritual impartation and empowerment to succeed to increase or prosper in order to fulfill a predetermined purpose or destiny.*

It must be noted that God did not curse mankind. The ground was cursed for man's sake.[57] The ground is considered man's "work place". The curse, as mentioned above, is directed at man's ability to be fruitful and productive as it pertains to his ability to prosper in the things he puts his hands to. The earth and every creature was created for man. God waited until the sixth day, after setting everything in its place, to bring man on

---

[57] Genesis 3:17

the scene. This is an indication that everything that proceeded man's arrival had a role in his ability to experience the fulfillment of his created purpose. The curse, as it relates to human beings, impacted our relationship with the earth. Even when God issued the curse concerning Cain's slaying of his brother Abel, the curse was again directed at the ground and his relationship to it. Specifically, the text reads:

> *"So now you are cursed from the earth, which has opened its mouth to receive your brother's blood from your hand. When you cultivate the ground, it will no longer yield its strength to you."*[58]

The curse that was placed upon Cain was *from* the earth. The result of this curse is a magnification of the previously issued curse found in Genesis 3:17. Cain's relationship with the ground was now completely severed instead of only being frustrated. Whatever he put his hands to in order to produce a living was destined to fail. It was cursed.

---

[58] Genesis 4:11-12

Like God, man has the ability to curse a thing with his words. Throughout scripture, we witness men speaking words of ill will toward other and their words coming to pass. Noah cursed his son Ham, which not only impacted Ham personally, but his generations.[59] Throughout the books of Leviticus, Numbers and Deuteronomy we are warned about the consequences of cursing and the reality of curses gaining entrance into ones life. Contrary to superstition, curses are not casual happenings that you stumble upon. The Bible reminds us that there is "*no curse causeless.*"[60] This means that all curses have a root cause and must be given access, permission and authorization by someone possessing authority to issue the curse.

The Bible also makes it clear that no one can curse what God has declared blessed, or bless that which God had declared cursed. This is due to the fact that God is the source of all authority.[61] In the book of Numbers, Balak,

---

[59] Genesis 9:25.
[60] Proverbs 26:2
[61] Roman 13:1

the king of Moab, called upon Balaam to curse the people of God because he feared them due to their number and proximity to his people. He said to Balaam:

" Therefore please come at once, curse this people for me, for they are too mighty for me. Perhaps I shall be able to defeat them and drive them out of the land, for I know that he whom you bless is blessed, and he whom you curse is cursed. "[62]

Remember, that a curse is an empowerment to fail. King Balak was asking Balaam to speak failure over the people of God. However, there was a problem. God had already declared them blessed!

When Balaam began to mediate on what to speak over the people, God intervened and told Balaam to go back to king Balak and say:

"How shall I curse whom God has not cursed? And how can I denounce whom the LORD has not denounced? "As I see him from the top of the rocks, And I look at him from the hills; Behold, a people {who} dwells apart, And will not be reckoned among the nations. "Who can

---

[62] Numbers 22:6

count the dust of Jacob, Or number the fourth part of Israel? Let me die the death of the upright, And let my end be like his!" Then Balak said to Balaam, "What have you done to me? I took you to curse my enemies, but behold, you have actually blessed them!" He replied, "Must I not be careful to speak what the LORD puts in my mouth?"[63]

Balak tried to force Balaam to curse the people of God on several occasions with the same result – he ended up blessing them instead. Remember, no one can bestow upon another what they do not possess. If they do not possess the authority to do a thing, then their words are empty and of no effect. God is the source of all authority. Therefore, a man or any other being cannot curse what He has blessed. This should give every child of God comfort in the midst of the evil times we live. Nothing can undo the blessing that God has declared over your life as a child of His and a citizen of His Kingdom. The enemy may not like it, but he and his kingdom are bound by the laws established by God.

---

[63] Numbers 23:7-12

Reversing the Curse

In closing this section of our study of the Law of Blessing and Cursing, I believe it is important to point out another aspect of this law that does not necessarily have to do with our tongues but directly impacts our everyday lives. This aspect of blessing and curse has to do with their influence in our lives as born again believers and citizens of God's Kingdom.

As mentioned earlier, the primary impact of the blessing and curse upon man was its impart on his ability to be fruitful and productive. Specifically, the curse caused our relationship with our work place to become more difficult. Sin gave cause to the curse and introduced into man's efforts to be productive pain, sorrow and insufficiency. The curse caused the earth to occupy a position in its relationship with man, that it was not originally created to occupy. It was created to serve man, not for man to serve it.

As a consequence of the curse, man had to now serve the ground in order to receive what he needed, instead of the ground freely providing him what he needs.

He Became a Curse

In the book of Galatians, Paul points out that Jesus became a curse for us.[64] I mentioned earlier in this chapter that man was not cursed - it was the ground that was cursed. Sin caused not only the curse that was placed upon the ground but the judgment of man. The consequence of the judgment was the carrying out of God's declared punishment for disobedience – spiritual death. When man broke God's law, the "judgment" for the trespass was immediately carried out. Man spiritually died on the spot, which severed his relationship with God. In addition, when God cursed the ground, it disrupted our relationship with it. Therefore, in order for Christ to fully deal with the consequences of

---

[64] Galatians 3:13

man's sin and restore him to his original position, He had to address our relationship with God and the earth.

We know that Christ sacrificial and redemptive work on the cross redeemed us from the death sentence we received. His blood paid the price for our sins. As a result, we now have access, through faith in Jesus Christ, to the Father just like Adam had. As born again sons of God, He presently lives within us in the person of the Holy Spirit. We have been completely restored to the same position Adam had before the fall .in our relationship with God and the earth.

Operation Restoration

A less known fact, that is just as important to our having dominion, is that Christ came to not only restored our relationship with God our Father, but also with the earth as well. God gave man "dominion" over the earth. However, due to the fall, the earth was authorized to withhold from man what he needed. Therefore, in order for our restoration to be complete, the Savior would have to address the curse that was placed upon the ground as well. This aspect of the Savior's work was expected and understood at a very early stage of man's history. The Bible records in Genesis 5:29 that:

> *"Lamech lived one hundred and eighty-two years, and had a son. And he called his name Noah, saying, "This one will comfort us concerning our work and the toil of our hands, because of the ground which the Lord has cursed."*

The people were looking for a savior, who would restore their relationship with the ground. They thought this savior was Noah. They expected the Savior to reverse the curse that was causing them to be unproductive in their work. It is likely, that it was passed down through the generation to Lamech how Adam and Eve did not serve the ground. Prior to the fall they could walk up to a tree and the tree would immediately provide them its fruit upon command without delay.

Whatever the case may have been, they understood that the ground did not always respond to man in the manner it now did. This text establishes that one the expected works of the "'Savior" was that He would restore man's relationship and dominion over the ground.

This is why the Book of Galatians reveals that Jesus became a curse for man on the cross. By becoming a curse for us, Jesus destroyed the right of the ground to withhold anything from us as sons of God. As spiritual sons of God, we now have the same rights Adam had to have his needs met without the requirement of toil and labor.

Jesus said in Matthew 6:33, that those who seek first the Kingdom of God and His righteousness, will have all their needs *provided* them. The "things" that Jesus spoke of were such things as food, drink, clothing and our health. These are the very things that the vast majority of people spend their days working for. The text did not say that it would be given to them as wages or after they've earned them. No! These things are *given or provided* them in response to their relationship with God and His Kingdom. This current system of work and of "earning a living" is a remnant of the curse and a result of their being an absence of the knowledge of the Kingdom.

This is why Jesus could walk up to a fig tree, when the Bible declares that it was *not time for figs* and demand that it yield its fruit for Him upon His command. Why? Because He was operating in the capacity of the Second Adam, who had no sin and therefore, not subject to the curse. As a result, the tree had no legal right to withhold from Him what He requested. As born again sons of God, we have our righteousness through the same Jesus who knew there was nothing that disqualified Him from having what He needed provided to Him without Him having to serve the ground for it.

To see this more clearly, lets take a look at the text. Mark chapter 11 reads in pertinent part:

> *"Now the next day, when they had come out from Bethany, He was hungry. And seeing from afar a fig tree having leaves, He went to see if perhaps He would find something on it. When He came to it, He found nothing but leaves, for*

it was not the season for figs. In response Jesus said to it, "Let no one eat fruit from you ever again." And His disciples heard it.' ... 'When evening had come, He went out of the city. Now in the morning, as they passed by, they saw the fig tree dried up from the roots. And Peter, remembering, said to Him, "Rabbi, look! The fig tree which You cursed has withered away."[65]

The text plainly states that it was not the season for figs, but yet Jesus expected it to produce what He requested. Being a man in right relationship with God, and the power to bless or curse, Jesus exercised dominion over the tree and decreed its destiny by authoritatively speaking to it. Again, I must reiterate that, as spirit filled born again believers, we too are sons of God who are in right standing with Him through the righteousness we possess in Jesus Christ.

In summary, Jesus' blood took care of the separation between man and God. It removed the stain of sin making us acceptable to God again. Jesus became a curse to address the curse that was placed upon the

---

[65] Mark 11:12-14, 20-21.

ground which directly impacted man's ability to fulfill his mandate of dominion given him by God. By becoming a curse, Jesus restored man's relationship with the earth.

 We are not confined to the world's way of doing things nor this system that is governed by the curse. We have been restored in every respect. In our relationship with God and the ground!

The Earth Groans

Finally, in Romans chapter 8, Paul articulates the consequence of Jesus becoming a curse for man and restoring his relationship with the earth. Paul reveals not only was man since the days of Noah, expecting the Savior to restore man's relationship with the earth, but the earth itself also was expecting deliverance from the consequences of the curse. Specifically, the text reads:

> *For the earnest expectation of the creation
> eagerly waits for the revealing of the sons of
> God. For the creation was subjected to futility,
> not willingly, but because of Him who subjected*

it in hope; because the creation itself also will be delivered from the bondage of corruption into the glorious liberty of the children of God. For we know that the whole creation groans and labors with birth pangs together until now.[66]

This text is referencing the curse that God placed upon the ground, not because of any fault of its own, but because God commanded it to. As mentioned previously, the earth was created to serve man and provide for his needs, not for man to serve the ground in order for his needs to be met. Therefore, due to the earth's inability to fulfill it purpose it was placed in bondage because of the curse unable to fulfill its creative purposes.

The text explains that the earth was awaiting the arrival of, what Paul called, "sons or children of God". These are human beings who are spiritually restored in their relationship with God and occupy the same position Adam did prior to the fall in his relationship with God and the earth. The curse was empowered by sin. Jesus having no sin and being the corporal representative of all

---

[66] Romans 8:19-22

mankind effectively restored and redeemed all who would stand in His righteousness.

The earth has been waiting throughout history for the moment when God's Kingdom would again be occupied by spirit filled and spirit led sons who have the ability to relate to God and the earth as they were created to do. This was not possible until Jesus came and destroyed the power of sin and the curse over man. This point is emphasized the last words of verse 22, where it says - *"until now"*. It wasn't until Jesus finished His work on the cross and became a curse for mankind could man overcome the influence of the curse over the ground. The earth could finally declare that its rightful rulers again had dominion over it. These rulers are the sons of God – the other speaking spirits.

The Law of the Tongue

Personal Confession

I am a Believer, I believe the Word of God.

I walk by faith, and not by sight.

Faith comes by hearing, and hearing the Word of God.

I seek first the Kingdom of God, therefore,

I am fully supplied in all things.

I call upon the harvest, of every good seed sown,

in the name of Jesus.

For God delights in my prosperity.

I can do exceedingly, abundantly,

above all that I could ask or think,

according to the power, that works in me.

I am anointed, and highly favored by God.

I will not faint, nor fear any evil,

because I have already prevailed!

It is so – in Jesus name – Amen!

The Law of the Tongue

About the Author

Dr. J.C. Matthews is a noted author, teacher, speaker and the visionary founding Pastor of Dunamis Life Ministries of Dallas, Texas. Dr. Matthews is known for his love of God's Word, wisdom and gift for practically applying scripture to everyday life. He has authored several books and is a noted devotional writer for various Christian media outlets.

Dr. Matthews possesses a B.A. in Political Science, as well as a Juris Doctorate (J.D.) degree. While in law school J.C. was twice recognized for his outstanding study of law by his induction into the "Who's Who Among American Law Students". He has also been honored as an Urban All-American by the General Assembly of the Ohio State Senate.

Dr. Matthews lives in the Dallas / Ft. Worth Texas area with his wife Gena and four children.

To contact or schedule Pastor Matthews please do so by visiting www.jcmatthewsminitries.com.

Also Available

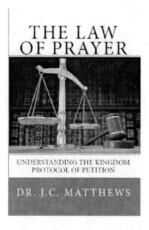

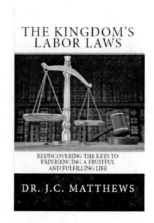

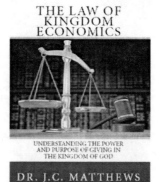

Check out www.blessedbookspublishing.com or www.jcmatthewsministries.com for more titles from this series for dates of release and availability.

Here are more titles by Dr. J.C. Matthews.

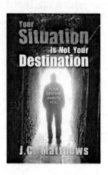 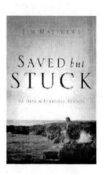

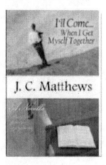 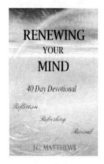

For more information concerning other resources offered
by J.C. Matthews, please visit:

www.jcmatthewsministries.com

CPSIA information can be obtained at www.ICGtesting.com
Printed in the USA
LVOW04s0142220813

349087LV00023B/284/P